S · T · E · P

# *Home*



Dave Boyle
Wendy Pitt

CAMBRIDGE
UNIVERSITY PRESS

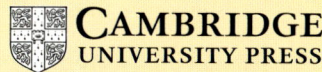

Published by the Press Syndicate of the University of Cambridge
The Pitt Building, Trumpington Street, Cambridge CB2 1RP
40 West 20th Street, New York, NY 10011–4211, USA
10 Stamford Road, Oakleigh, Victoria 3166, Australia

In association with Staffordshire County Council

© Cambridge University Press 1992

First published 1992

Printed in Great Britain by Scotprint Limited, Musselburgh

Designed and Produced by Gecko Limited, Bicester, Oxon.

A catalogue record for this book is available from the British Library.

ISBN 0 521 40624 2

PICTURE ACKNOWLEDGEMENTS

Beamish Open Air Museum 16.
Christopher Coggins 10, 12, 20, 31.
Robert Harding Picture Library 17t, 25cr, 25cl, 25br, 27bc, 32.
Images 7, 27bl.
Rob Judges 17b, 24br, 24–5tc.
Andrew Lawson 25tr, 27br.
Lego UK Ltd. 8.
Linda Proud 24tl, 24cr.
Zefa Ltd. 17cr.
Codsall Middle School, Staffs, for the model on page 20

Picture Research by Linda Proud

NOTICE TO TEACHERS

The contents of this book are in the copyright of Cambridge University Press. Unauthorised copying of any of the pages is not only illegal but also goes against the interests of the authors.

For authorised copying please check that your school has a licence (through the Local Education Authority) from the Copyright Licensing Agency which enables you to copy small parts of the text in limited numbers.

# Contents

| | |
|---|---|
| **Homes** | **4** |
| **Rooms** | **16** |
| **The garden** | **24** |

# Homes

## Talking together

How many different types of home can you see in the picture?
How are they different? How are they the same?
Why are they different?
How could you group the homes in the picture?
Can you think of any other types that are not shown?

What materials are they made from?
How were they built?
How does a home get water, electricity and gas?
What happens to sewage?

How have homes changed over the years?

Find out what homes are like in different parts of the world.

# The need

Imagine a building society is holding a competition for young people to design their ideal home of the future. Your school has entered this competition.

# Developing your design

These houses were being built in 1992. What would be different in your house?

## Planning your work

What would your ideal home look like?

What would be special about it?

Which materials would you build it from?

Why would you use those materials?

Where would you build it?

### • DATA FILE •
**Research:** data collection and display

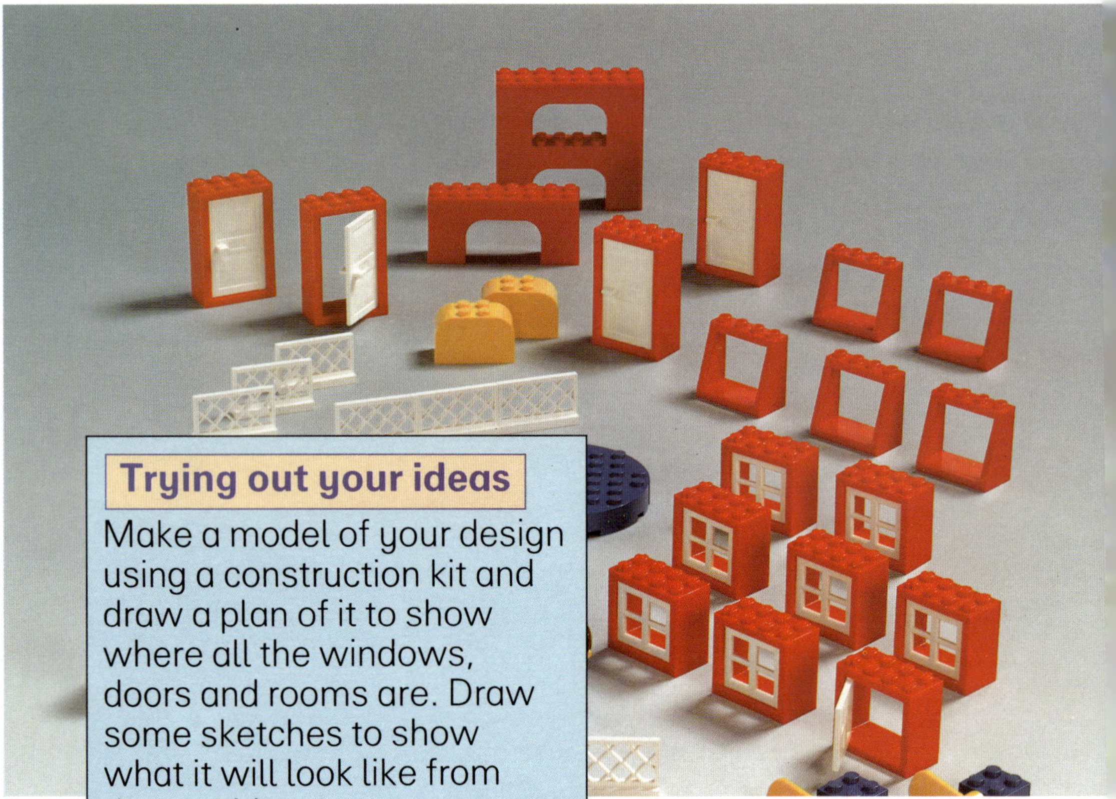

### Trying out your ideas

Make a model of your design using a construction kit and draw a plan of it to show where all the windows, doors and rooms are. Draw some sketches to show what it will look like from the outside.

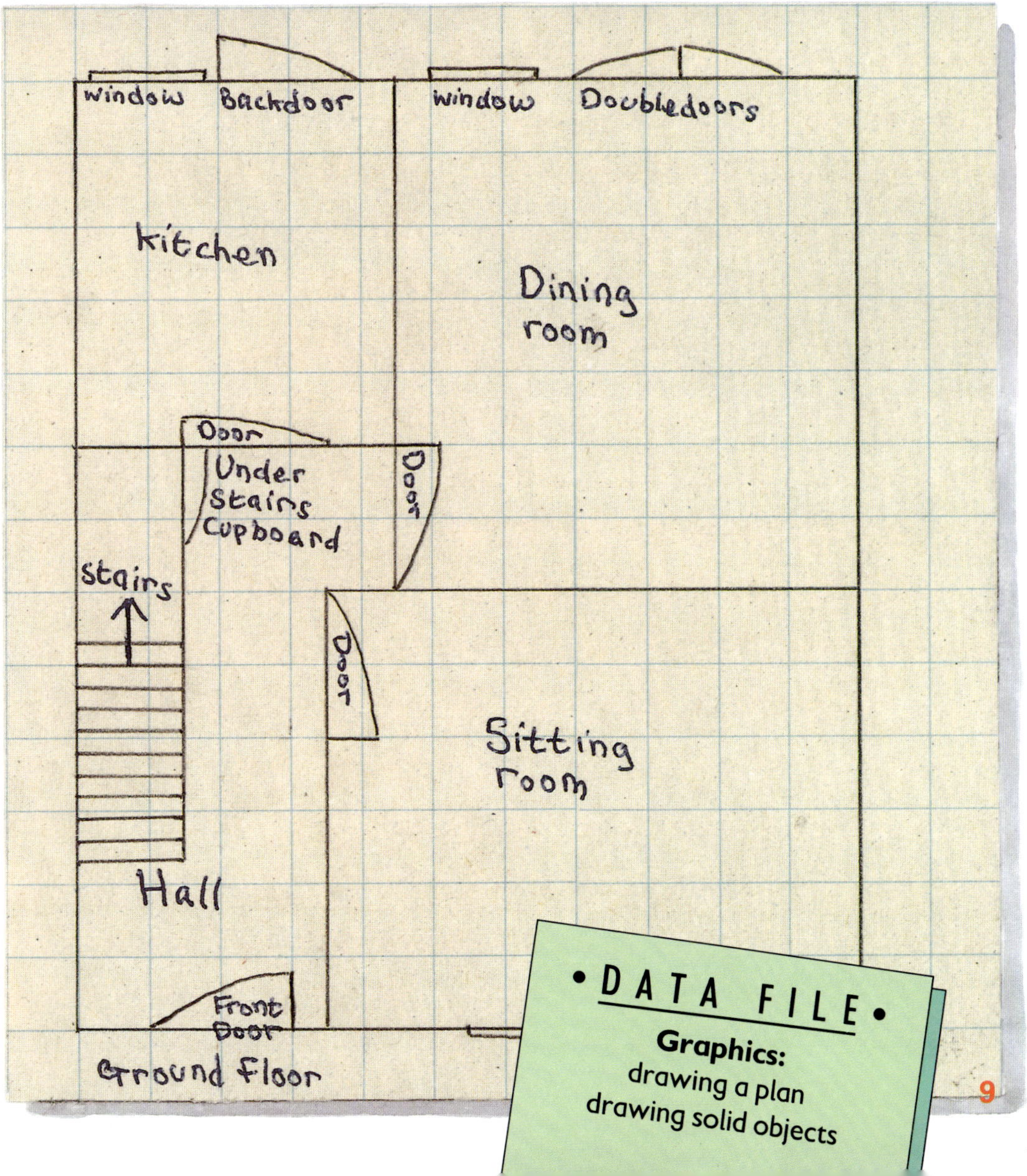

## • DATA FILE •
**Graphics:**
drawing a plan
drawing solid objects

## A model home

When you are happy with your ideas try and make a model using card. To give you an idea of the size, use some model vehicles and model people.

You will need to
- mark out a net using scrap card. If you are not sure how to do this open out some old cardboard boxes to see how they have been made.

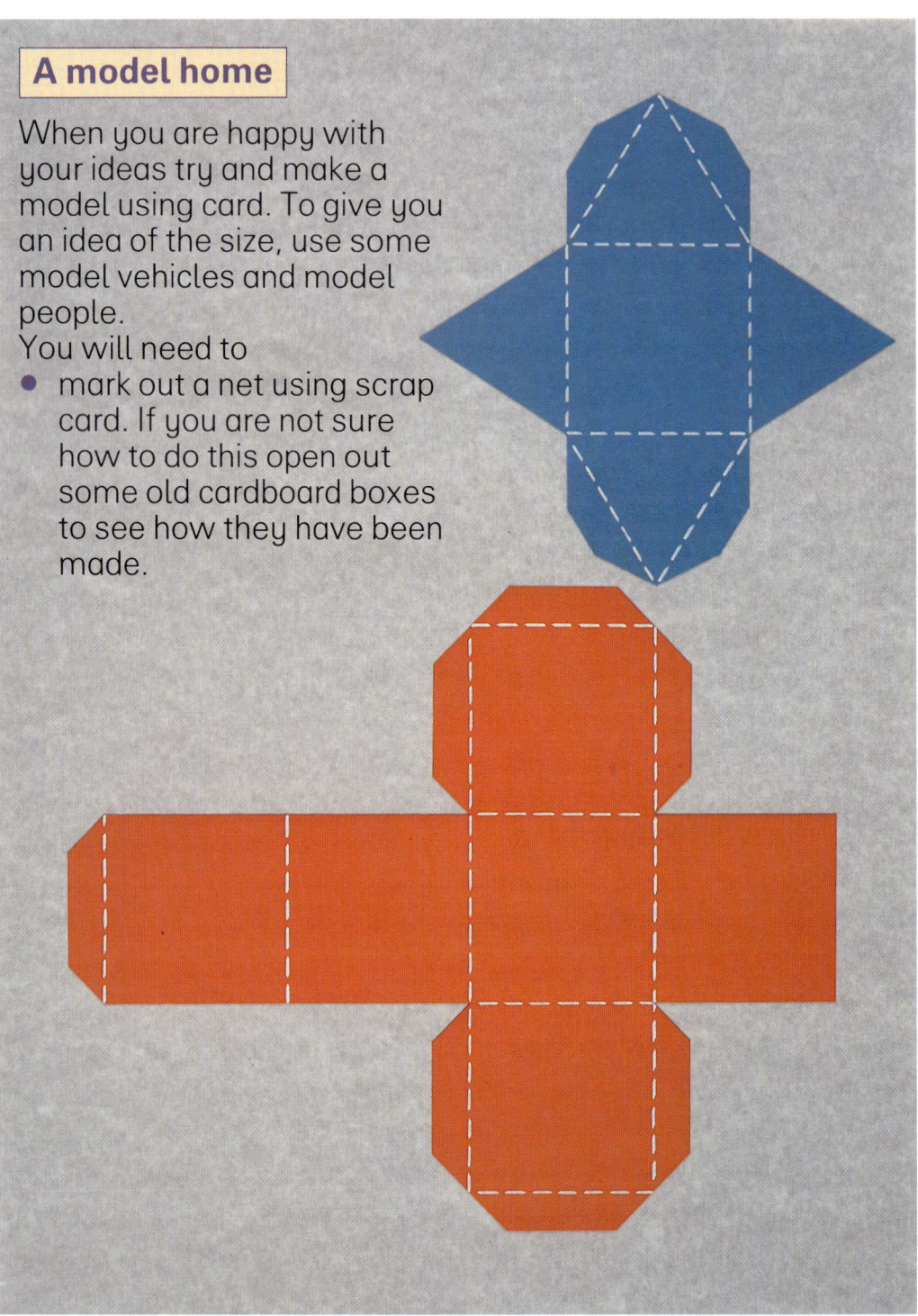

- mark and cut out windows and doors while the card is flat before glueing it together.

If you are making a complex shape you may need to make it in parts and then join them together. By having a removable roof you could also show the rooms inside.

To make your model more interesting you might like to have lighting and moving parts.

• D A T A   F I L E •

**Card and paper:**
cutting
folding and strengthening
joining
nets

## Ideas for lighting

**· DATA FILE ·**

**Electricity:**
simple circuits 1
simple circuits 2
switches 1

A switch for one bulb

# Ideas for moving parts

## A hinge

## A sliding mechanism

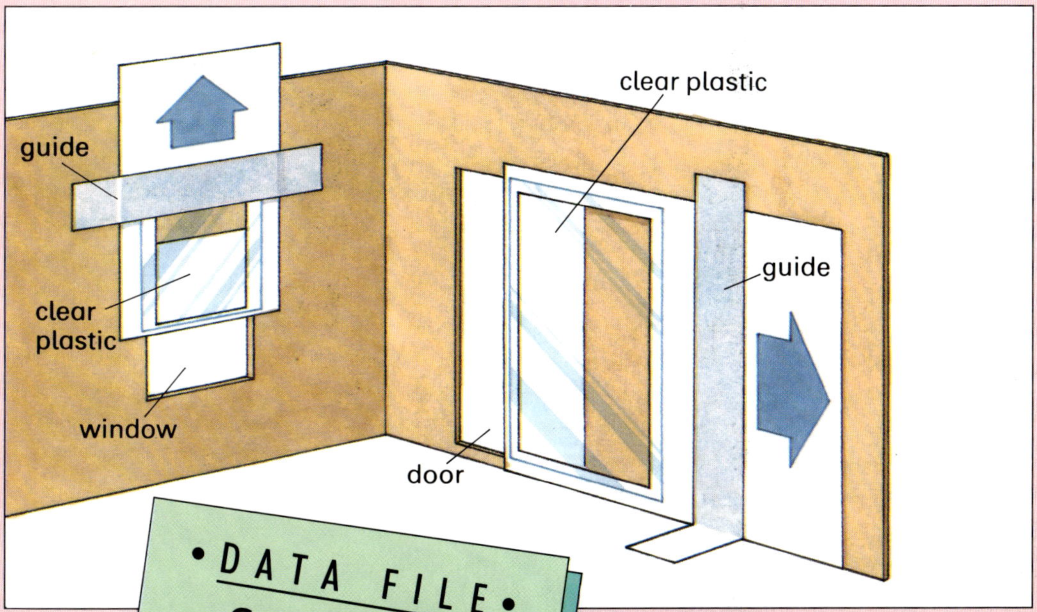

• DATA FILE •
**Card and paper:** mechanisms

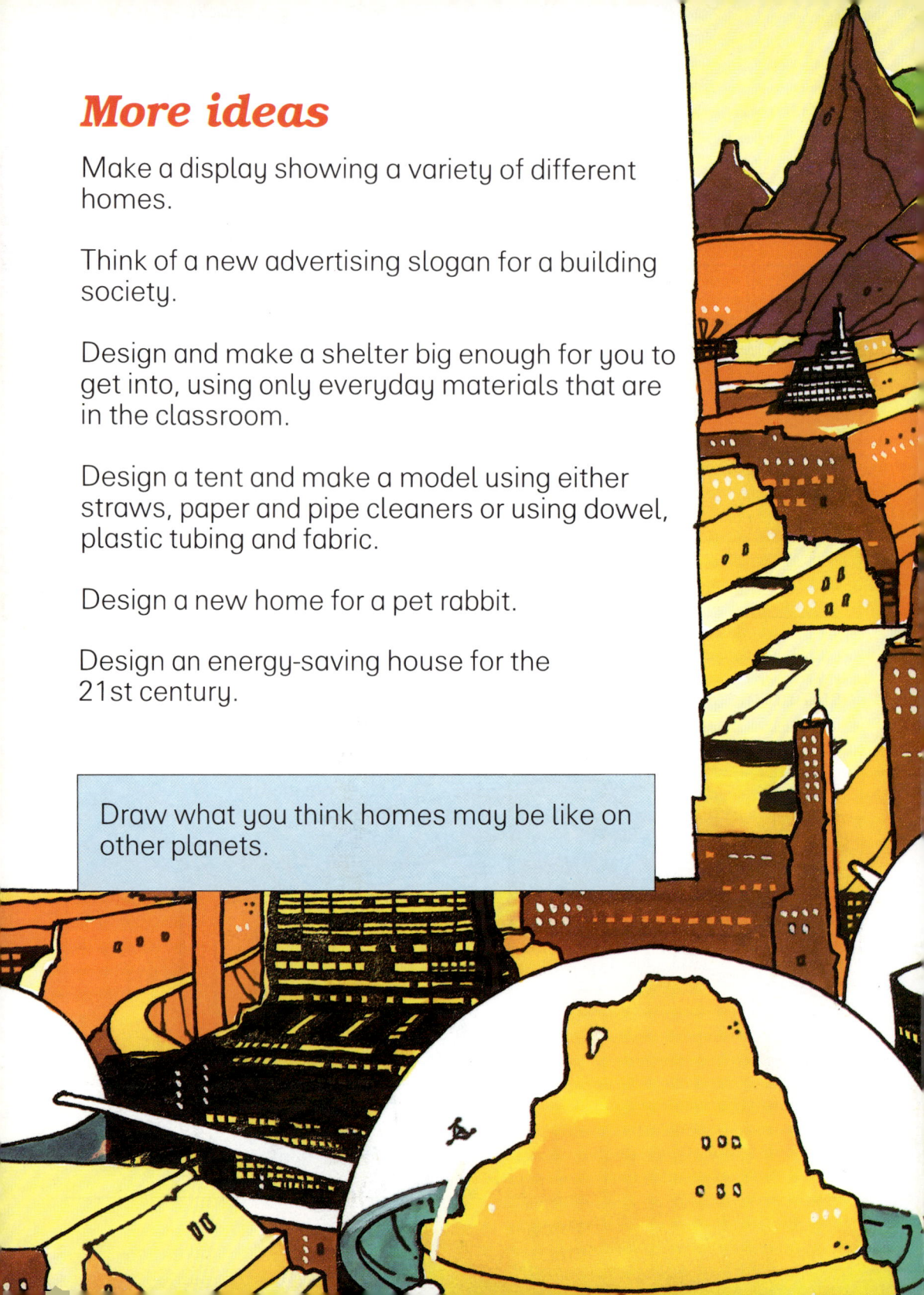

# More ideas

Make a display showing a variety of different homes.

Think of a new advertising slogan for a building society.

Design and make a shelter big enough for you to get into, using only everyday materials that are in the classroom.

Design a tent and make a model using either straws, paper and pipe cleaners or using dowel, plastic tubing and fabric.

Design a new home for a pet rabbit.

Design an energy-saving house for the 21st century.

Draw what you think homes may be like on other planets.

# Rooms

## Talking together

What sort of rooms can be found in a home?
What are they used for?
What is different about them?
What is the same?

What sort of furniture is used in each room?

How does the use of a room affect the furniture and decoration?

How have rooms changed over the years?
Look at the pictures to help you?

Why is the lighting sometimes different in each room?

What different methods of heating can be used?

Victorian nursery

1940s

# Developing your design

## Making a room plan

Make a plan of your room showing all the doors and windows. Mark the position of any power points and wall lights.

Decide what furniture you will need. Don't forget things like storage space, work surfaces and lamps.

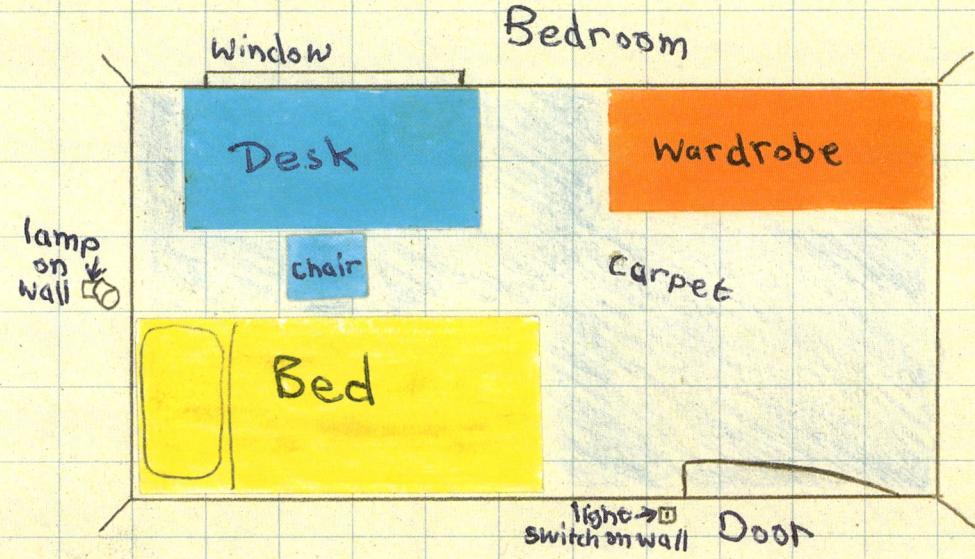

Make card cut-outs of the furniture and try them in different positions on your plan.

Once you are happy with this think about the colours you want for the carpet, walls, paintwork, curtains and furniture.

Now you are ready to make a model of your ideas.

• D A T A   F I L E •
**Graphics:**
drawing a plan
**Card and paper:**
nets

## A model room

An old cardboard box could be furnished and equipped using scraps of wallpaper, carpet, and card or timber furniture. It may look even better if you could show the lighting using a circuit.
Model people and pictures may make your model room look more realistic.

# Working with fabric

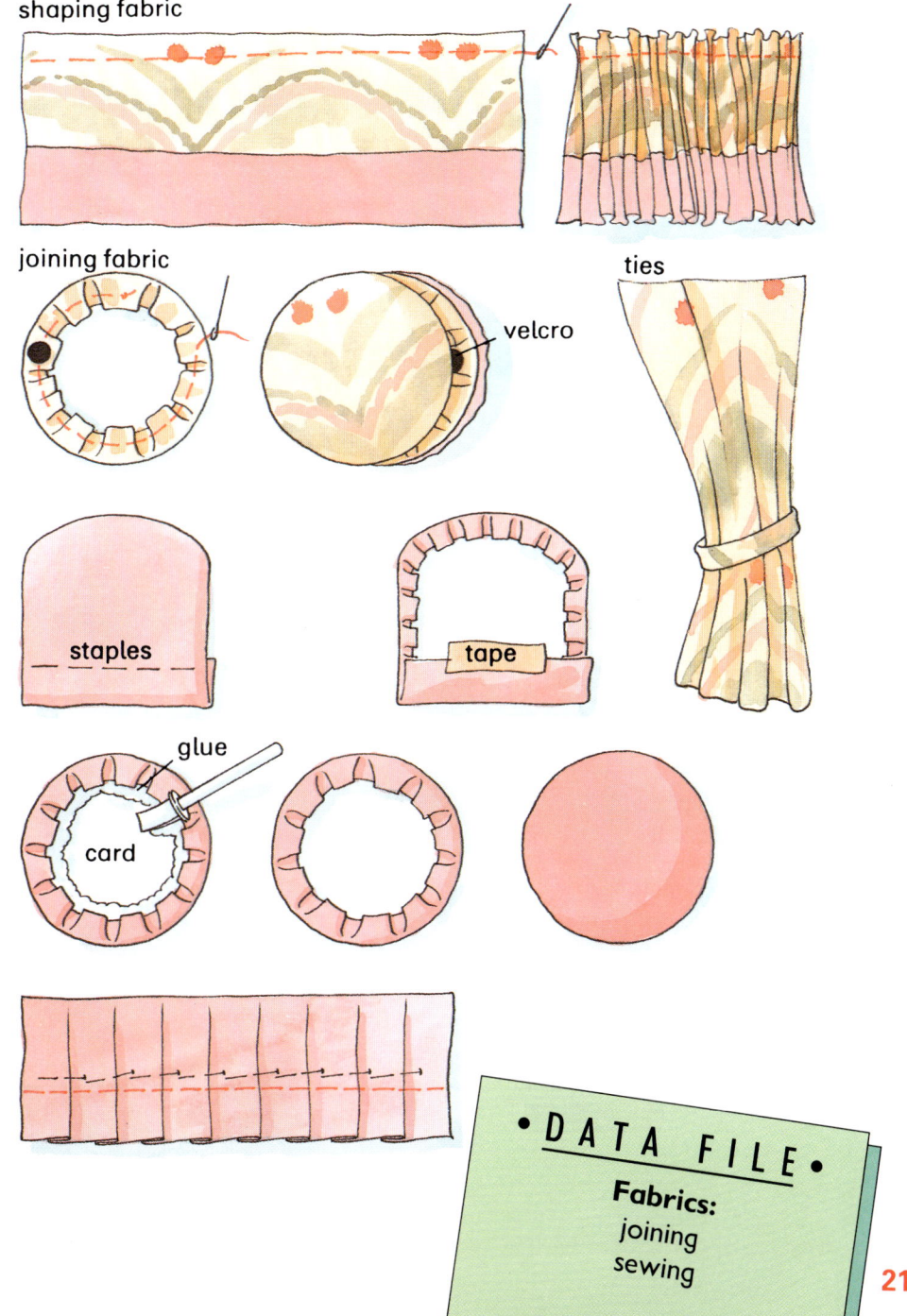

shaping fabric

joining fabric

ties

velcro

staples

tape

glue

card

**· DATA FILE ·**
**Fabrics:**
joining
sewing

## Ideas for printing

## Ideas for simple circuits

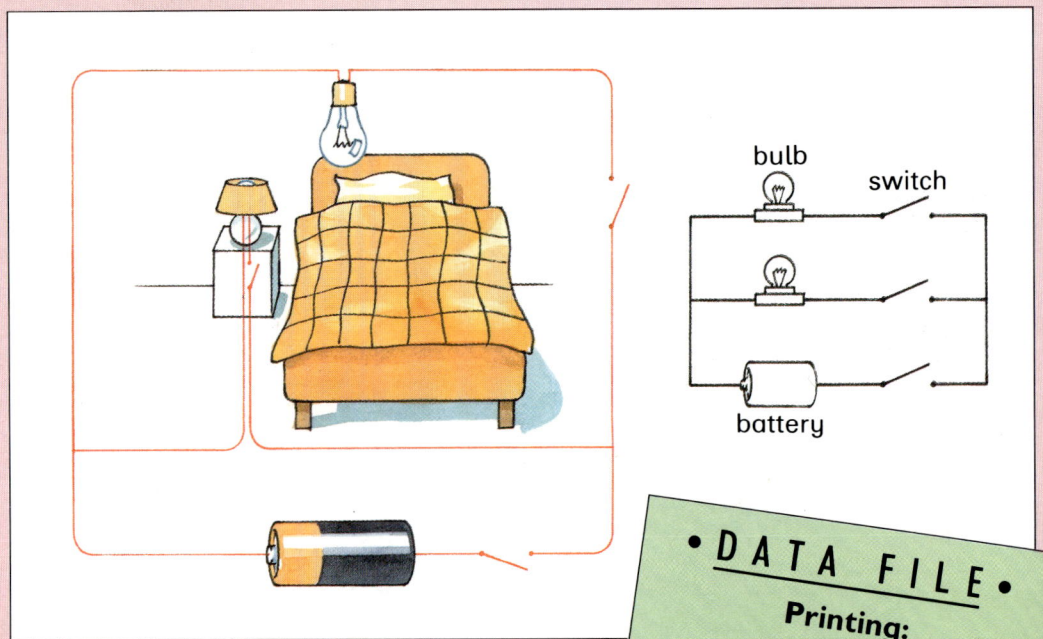

bulb
switch
battery

• D A T A  F I L E •

**Printing:**
using potatoes
using blocks and rollers
**Electricity:**
simple circuits 1 and 2
switches 1 and 2

22

# More ideas

Design and make a model of a storage unit to hold a music centre with space for all your records, tapes and compact discs.

Design and print some wallpaper for your room.

Design and make a lighting system which can be changed to suit your moods.

Design and make some cushion covers for your room.

Make a display of flowers or plants to brighten up a room.

Devise a system to keep your room clean and tidy.

How could you store
- books
- shoes
- pencils, pens and paper
- toys

# The Garden

## Talking together

> Make a collection of garden pictures from magazines and catalogues

How many different types of garden can you think of?

What makes each one special?
What do they all have in common?
What makes them different?

What things would you have in your ideal garden?

# The need

Imagine the garden in your new home is in an awful mess, full of rubble and overgrown with plants. It will need clearing and redesigning. How would you design your ideal garden?

# *Developing your design*

## Planning your work

What are your favourite flowers, plants, trees and vegetables?

What makes a garden interesting? Think about the position of paths, seats, ponds and shelters.

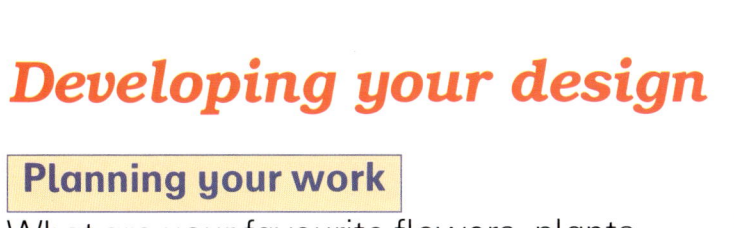

Is any special equipment needed for children, pets, barbecues or for drying clothes? Is anything special needed for people with disabilities?

**· DATA FILE ·**
**Research:** data collection and display

# A model garden

Which materials would you need to model your ideal garden?

What different ways are there of putting a boundary around a garden?

Are there any special buildings found in gardens?

How could your garden waste be recycled?

Could your garden be used to encourage wildlife?

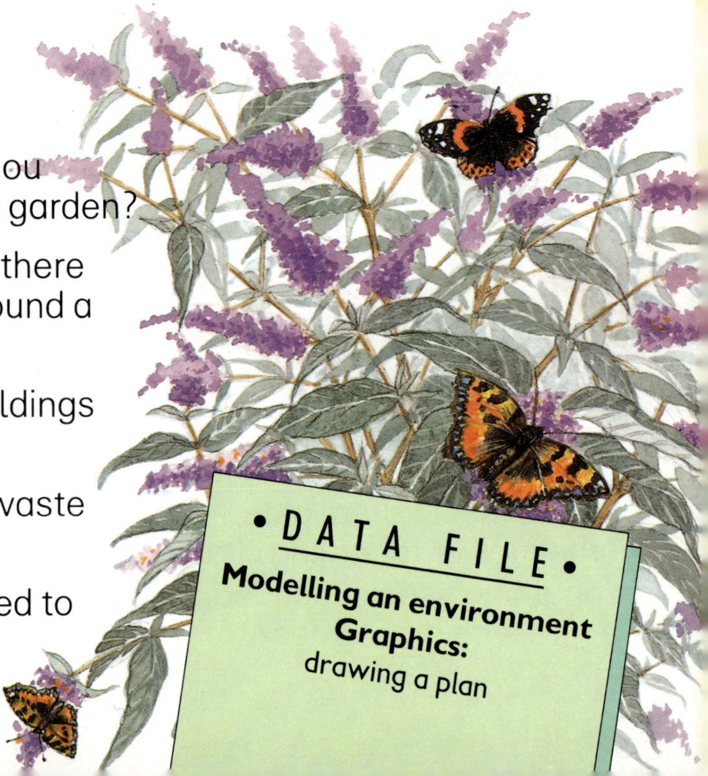

• DATA FILE •
**Modelling an environment
Graphics:**
drawing a plan

## Trying out your ideas

Use a construction kit to experiment with the layout or plan your ideas with card cut-outs on a map of your garden.

You may be able to use computer programs like Logo or Paintspa to try out your ideas.

## A model garden

Make a model of the garden using everyday materials such as paper, card, wood, plasticine and fabric.

## Using papier mâché

Paste small pieces of paper onto shapes made from screwed-up paper, plasticine or a framework of wire.

• **D A T A   F I L E** •
Modelling an environment
Papièr mâché
Collage, montage and decoupage
Finishes
Wood

## Ideas for textures and surfaces

painting glass paper for grass

carpet

painting corrugated cardboard

## Making structures from wood

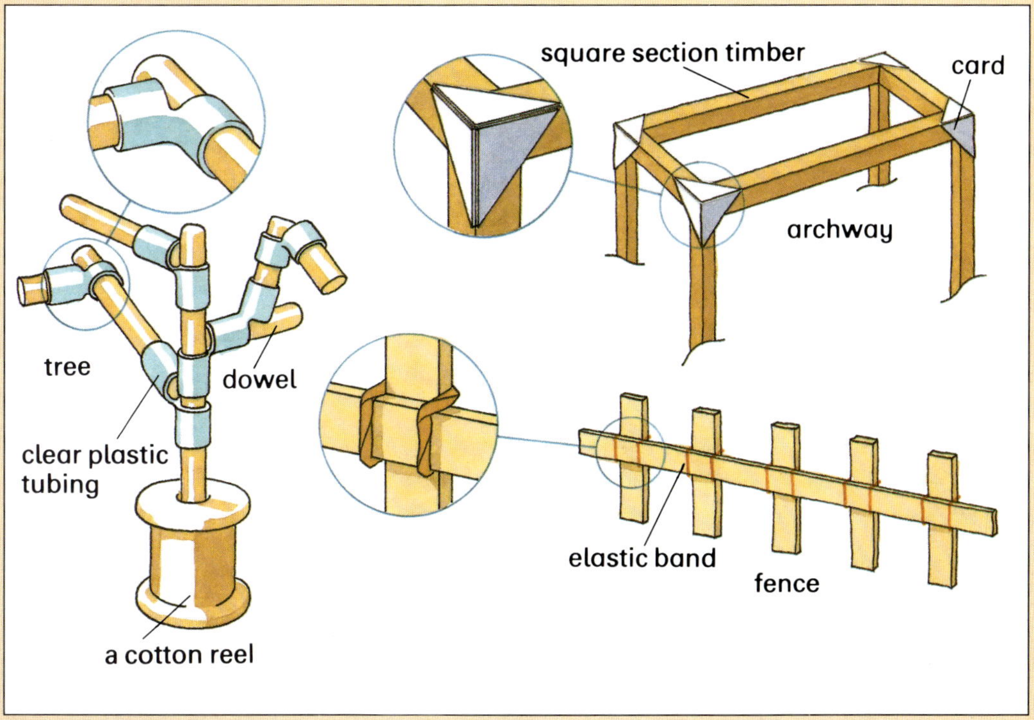

square section timber

card

archway

tree

dowel

clear plastic tubing

elastic band

fence

a cotton reel

31

# More ideas

Design and make some models of patio furniture.

Plan a section of the garden for a partially sighted person.

Plan a menu for a barbecue for your friends.

How could the garden be lit for the evening?

Plan a vegetable garden which could help to reduce the family food bill.

Design a flower bed to commemorate a special event.